Snap Happy

Alison Hawes
Illustrated by Mike Phillips

RIGBY

I had a camera.
I wanted to take photos of Anna on her wedding day.

Mr Flash had a camera.
He wanted to take photos of Anna on her wedding day too.

I took a photo of Anna and my dad.
So did Mr Flash.

Anna said, “I am so happy!”
Dad said, “I am happy too!”
Mr Flash didn’t say anything.
He didn’t look happy.

I took a photo of Anna and Mike.
So did Mr Flash.

Mike said, "I am so happy!"
I said, "I am happy too!"
Mr Flash didn't say anything.
He still didn't look happy.

Mr Flash put his photos in a book.
When we looked at the photos, I was in the way in all of them!

Anna said, "I am so sad."
Mr Flash said, "I am so mad!"

I didn't say anything.

I put my photos in a book.

Anna and I looked at the photos.
Anna said, "I love your photos!
They make me so happy!"